Retail Reimagined

Leveraging Blockchain for Customer Experience and Supply Chain

Table of Contents

Chapter 1. Introduction

In this special report, "Retail Reimagined: Leveraging Blockchain for Customer Experience and Supply Chain," we delve into an innovative crossroads of technology and commerce. Although the topic may seem complex, we assure you it's more exciting than it seems at first glance! We've broken down the intricate world of blockchain into easily digestible pieces, presenting it as a powerful tool to dramatically enhance both the customer experience and the efficiency of supply chains in the retail world. This report, while deeply informative, is presented in practical language that makes the tech-savvy subject palatable for everyone, from beginner to expert. Not only does it presents an intriguing blend of cutting-edge technology with retail business essentials, it also offers a blueprint for how retailers could reimagine their operations. Diving into the report is a sure way to get ahead of the curve and inject innovation into your business. You are just a purchase away from accessing essential insights that could transform your retail strategies!

Chapter 2. Understanding Blockchain: The Basics

Blockchain technology has risen to prominence due to its central role in the operation of cryptocurrencies, most notably Bitcoin. However, the applications of blockchain extend far beyond digital currencies alone. The ability to securely verify transactions and records offers numerous opportunities for businesses, particularly in the retail sector where supply chain veracity and customer experience can be greatly enhanced.

2.1. The Concept of Blockchain

The fundamental concept of a blockchain is quite straightforward. Essentially, a blockchain is a specific type of database, used primarily for recording transactions. However, what differentiates it from a traditional database is its unique ability to cryptographically secure and link blocks of transactions.

Imagine a chain of blocks, where each block contains a list of transactions. Every time a new transaction occurs, it is added to the next block in the chain. Once the block is completed, it is linked to the previous block, creating the 'chain' in 'blockchain'. The critical component in securing these blocks together is the cryptographic 'hash'. A hash is a mathematical algorithm that transforms any block of data into a short, fixed series of numbers and letters. Each block's hash is unique and based on the transactions within it. Furthermore, each block's hash includes part of the previous block's hash, linking them together and making the blockchain tamper-proof.

2.2. Blockchain: Decentralized and Secure

A key characteristic of blockchain technology is its decentralized nature. Blockchain operates on a network of computers, also known as nodes, with each node having a copy of the entire blockchain. This decentralization makes blockchain incredibly secure since altering a transaction requires a majority of the nodes to agree on the change. This consensus mechanism ensures that no single entity controls the blockchain, and the likelihood of fraud or manipulation is significantly reduced.

2.3. Transparency: A Pinnacle Feature of Blockchain

One of the major advantages of blockchain is transparency. The nature of a blockchain's distributed ledger means that it is an open, decentralized database. Everyone in the network can see all the transactions. Yet, while it may seem paradoxical, this transparency does not compromise user privacy. Although transactions are viewable, they are recorded via unique codes rather than personal identifiers. Thus the blockchain maintains transparency while also protecting user privacy, boosting both trust and security.

2.4. Smart Contract: The Game Changer

Blockchain technology also facilitates the use of 'smart contracts'. These are self-executing contracts with the terms of the agreement between buyer and seller being directly written into lines of code. Since these codes are distributed across the decentralised blockchain network, they get automatically executed when the agreed conditions are met. This saves the time normally spent on paperwork and traditional contract validation, and also significantly reduces the possibility of dispute.

2.5. A Look Inside Blockchain's Proof-of-Work

Proof-of-work is a consensus mechanism employed by blockchain systems to approve transactions and add them to the public ledger. In essence, this system requires participants, known as 'miners', to solve a complex mathematical problem. The first one who solves the problem gets to add the new block of transactions to the chain. Notably, proof-of-work not only maintains the integrity of the blockchain and prevents fraud, but it also ensures that no central authority can interfere with the transaction history.

2.6. Blockchain vs Traditional Systems: A Contrast

The blockchain technology dramatically contrasts with traditional systems in many key aspects. Unlike centralized databases that rely on a single authorities like banks or governments to verify and approve transactions, blockchain is decentralized, distributed, and transparent. This drastically increases security and removes the need for mediators, making peer-to-peer transactions more seamless and efficient. Moreover, through blockchain, retailers can create a more transparent and trustworthy relationship with their consumers while optimizing their supply chain processes.

In conclusion, the blockchain technology, with its ground-breaking features and benefits, offers a wealth of opportunities for the retail industry. It carries the potential to revolutionize operations, enhance the customer experience, and create a more efficient and transparent supply chain. By understanding the basics of blockchain, retailers can start to explore how they can leverage this technology to create a more profitable, competitive, and customer-centric business.

Chapter 3. Blockchain in Retail: An Overview

The integration of blockchain technology into the retail industry represents a pivotal shift in how businesses operate and customers experience shopping. With blockchain, retailers have a digital ledger that ensures greater transparency, security, and efficiency in transactions, solving significant issues associated with traditional transaction methods.

3.1. The Basics of Blockchain in Retail

Rooted firmly in cryptography, blockchain is essentially a decentralized database, also known as a distributed ledger. Each piece of information (or block) on the chain is timestamped and securely linked to the preceding and following data block, creating an unalterable, traceable line of transactions. This level of traceability can revolutionize the retail sector, a industry traditionally faced with challenges around transparency, supply chain inefficiency, counterfeit products, and customer loyalty.

3.2. The Role of Blockchain in Enhancing Customer Experience

Blockchain technology infuses numerous advantages into the retail customer experience. For one, it ensures heightened product authenticity. As every product journey from manufacturer to consumer is recorded on the digital ledger, customers gain access to an immutable product journey, ensuring authenticity and promoting brand trust. They know exactly where their product came from and the journey it took to reach them. This level of transparency is a significant step forward, especially in industries such as luxury goods or food where provenance matters.

Furthermore, blockchain can boost loyalty programs. Retailers can create blockchain-based tokens for loyalty rewards, providing an immutable and secure way of tracking points. This could help eliminate fraudulent claims and make it easier for customers to redeem and transfer points, improving overall customer engagement.

Lastly, micropayments via blockchain have also seen increasing adoption. By cutting out mediators, transactions, especially cross-border ones, can become faster, cheaper, and more efficient, enhancing customer convenience.

3.3. Blockchain Reinventing the Supply Chain

Traditional supply chain systems are often marred by inefficiencies, inaccuracies, and lack of transparency, leading to loss of trust and revenue. Blockchain can rectify this. Being immutable by design, a blockchain-powered supply chain offers full transparency, making it possible for all parties – manufacturers, vendors, logistics, retailers, and consumers – to trace a product's journey from production to final sale.

It also offers potential solutions for real-time tracking, eliminating inaccuracies and lengths of wait during transit. Smart contracts, or self-executing contracts with set rules, can automate various processes such as payments or order placement once conditions are met, increasing efficiency, and reducing the scope for disputes or delays.

3.4. Pitfalls and Challenges

While the blockchain promises a plethora of benefits, its implementation comes with its share of challenges. Firstly, the technology is still nascent, and many retailers lack the understanding and technical expertise for seamless adoption.

Secondly, blockchain's decentralized nature may lead to regulatory challenges. Without universally accepted regulations, issues around compliance could arise, delaying wider acceptance.

Lastly, the scalability of blockchain technology remains a concern. As the chain of data blocks grows longer, the infrastructure needed to maintain, process, and store the blockchain requires advanced hardware, raising questions about scalability in a retail environment, handling a large volume of transactions.

3.5. The Future Outlook

Despite the challenges, the future of blockchain in retail is promising. With increasing awareness, technological advancements, and regulatory evolution, retailers will continue to explore the potential of blockchain, capitalizing on the opportunities it presents.

In conclusion, the integration of blockchain technology into the retail industry can enforce improved customer loyalty, efficient supply chain management, and transparent product trails, easing manifold pressure points in the retail process. An understanding of how this technology fits into the retail landscape is essential in navigating the future evolution of the sector, playing a pivotal role in defining competitive advantage while improving customer experience and satisfaction.

Chapter 4. Peering into Customer Experience: Current State and Challenges

Customer experience transcends the bounds of simple transactions between buyers and sellers. It encapsulates the entirety of interactions a customer has with an organization, its offerings, and brand image across various touch points. In the age of digital transformation, customer experience has become pivotal in the sustainability and growth of organizations. E-commerce platforms and digital retail avenues are pushing boundaries and setting new expectations, making the retail landscape more challenging than ever before. This chapter will provide an in-depth look at the current state of customer experience in retail and highlight prevalent challenges that the retail sector is contending with.

4.1. The Current State of Customer Experience

Today's retail market is characterized by its highly competitive nature and the omnipresence of digital technologies. A shift, driven primarily by customers' increasing demands for personalized experiences, coupled with soaring competition from e-commerce giants, has altered the very crucible of customer experience.

In line with the global trend, customer experience has manifested itself as the differentiating frontier in retail. A report by Walker predicted that customer experience would overshadow price and product as the key brand differentiator by 2020. True to the forecast, retailers now compete more on services and the experiences they offer rather than merely on the product or price front.

Simultaneously, technology has assumed an ominous role within the customer experience landscape. In particular, the explosion of data and advent of artificial intelligence (AI) have worked in tandem to catalyze transformative changes, paving the way for unprecedented levels of personalization and customer insight.

4.2. Challenges Facing Customer Experience in Retail

However, this evolving landscape does not come without its quotas of challenges. Hence, for a deeper understanding, let's discuss some prominent customer experience roadblocks in retail.

4.3. Data Fragmentation

E-commerce has resulted in every customer interaction leaving a digital footprint, providing retailers a gold mine of data. However, with various interfaces that customers engage with—offline stores, online websites, mobile apps—the data generated is fragmented across channels. Integrating this data and decoding meaningful insights have posed significant challenges for the retail sector.

4.4. Personalization

As noted earlier, the demand for personalized experiences is at an all-time high. Retailers struggle to match the pace, often grappling with ineffective personalization systems that fail to deliver to customer expectations. Leveraging customer data for generating personal yet scalable experiences remains a tough nut to crack.

4.5. Trust and Security

With increasing data generation comes the increased responsibility of safeguarding customer information. Cybersecurity breaches and data thefts not only lead to huge financial losses but also severely damage a brand's reputation and customer trust.

4.6. Antiquated Supply Chains

Supply chain inefficiencies directly impact the customer's experience by causing delays in product delivery, inaccurate inventory details, and overall dissatisfaction. Antiquated supply chains lack visibility, agility, and real-time tracking—elements necessary in the current 'instantaneous' culture fostered by e-commerce giants.

4.7. Navigating the Omnichannel Landscape

Retailers find it difficult to offer consistent experiences across all customer touchpoints, both online and offline. The disparity in customer experiences often leads to lowered satisfaction and loyalty, impairing overall customer retention.

4.8. Integration of Innovative Technologies

In an era where machine learning, AI, and other advanced technologies dictate the development speed, retailers face the daunting task of integrating these into existing systems. Poor integration can result in disjointed services and disappointing customer experiences.

In summary, the retail industry today is at an imperative junction. On one hand, the changing customer expectations and technological influence point towards unexplored avenues of growth. On the other, these very factors present significant challenges, threatening customer experience standards. Understanding these challenges and developing strategies to overcome them will be paramount in defining the future customer experience in retail.

Chapter 5. Transforming Customer Experience with Blockchain

Blockchain technology, typically associated with financial transactions, has the potential to revolutionize the retail sector, specifically in driving customer experiences to whole new dimensions. In the age of the digital revolution, creating unforgettable customer experiences serves as the key differentiator for brands aiming to stay relevant and competitive.

5.1. Understanding Customer Experience

Customer Experience (CX) is the impression your customers have of your brand throughout all phases of the buyer's journey. It results from every interaction a customer has with your products and services, from navigation through your website to talking to customer service to receiving the product they've purchased. In a world where customer loyalty is hard to achieve, an excellent CX makes customers feel satisfied, valued, and therefore more likely to repeat purchases and recommend the brand to others.

Cryptocurrencies like Bitcoin and Ethereum immediately come to mind when we talk about blockchain, but the technology itself is far more versatile. It offers robust security, ensures transparency and traceability and promotes efficiency, all of which are ingredients for a stellar customer experience.

5.2. Tailoring Personalized Experiences with Blockchain

Delivering personalized experiences to customers has become paramount in today's digital age. Retailers are leveraging customer data to generate insights and drive more personalized interactions. Blockchain technology can foster this trend. It enables secure sharing of customer preference data among all parties involved in the customer journey. Retailers can utilize this info generated from an immutable source of truth to deliver precisely tailored products, benefits, and services to each customer.

In contrast to a traditional centralized database system, blockchain technology promotes secure and seamless data sharing. It ensures the customer's vital data stays tamper-proof, inspiring trust and confidence.

5.3. Enhancing Supply Chain Transparency with Blockchain

Transparency is another critical factor that contributes to customer experience. From product origin to understanding the business's ethical practices, customers today desire to access information about the products they choose to engage. The strongest advantage of blockchain technology is indeed its ability to provide transparency, while it also ensures data integrity.

By leveraging blockchain technology, retailers can track goods at each stage of their journey, from the manufacturer to the logistics provider to the store and, finally, to the customer. By doing so, they can provide customers with detailed information about a product's path, including its origins, quality checks it passed, whether ethical practices were followed, and so forth. Improved access to such data will prompt researchers to invest, thus contributing to better user experiences.

5.4. Blockchain Empowering Loyalty Programs

Loyalty programs have always been an effective way to retain customers and reward them for their brand loyalty. However, they can sometimes be complex and non-unified across different platforms. Blockchain offers a solution here as well.

Leveraging blockchain, brands can tokenize their loyalty points, making them more transparent and easy to manage for customers. Blockchain-based tokens are easy to track, and their value can be accurately determined, providing customers with a clear understanding of their loyalty program's worth. Customers can control their tokens securely in a blockchain-based digital wallet, eliminating the chance of expiry or loss.

Manufacturing consent from the customers, the retailers have the leverage to share loyalty tokens with partner brands, enhancing the user's value perception. This concept, known as 'Loyalty as a Service,' ensures a smooth, efficient, and interesting loyalty experience for the customers, thereby elevating the customer experience.

5.5. Securing Customer Data with Blockchain

While personalization and transparency are essential to customer experience, none would matter if customers feel their data are at risk. In the digital age, ensuring data privacy and security has become a prerequisite for a great customer experience.

Blockchain's fundamental design, which relies on cryptographic techniques, empowers it to offer unparalleled data security. With each transaction sealed in a 'block' and attached to the 'chain' permanently and unalterably, data manipulation or theft becomes implausible. Having such a secure system in place attributes to customer trust.

While blockchain technology still faces certain challenges such as misunderstandings about its nature and functionality, regulatory issues, and the need for standardization, it is rapidly gaining ground as a pivotal customer experience enhancer. Businesses ready to incorporate blockchain into their customer experience strategies now may reap substantial advantages over their competitors in the foreseeable future.

In conclusion, blockchain has the potential to transform the customer experience in retail entirely. It can deliver tailored experiences, provide unparalleled supply chain transparency, revolutionize loyalty programs, and secure customer data like never before. Retailers who recognize and act upon this will undoubtedly lead the next wave of customer experience innovation.

This ends our deep dive into how blockchain technology can reshape the retail sector by transforming customer experiences. The possibilities are exciting, and the next chapters will explore the applications of blockchain technology in the supply chain and beyond. The future of retail lies at this exciting juncture where technology and innovative customer service intersect. Let's ride this wave of transformation together!

Chapter 6. Decoding Supply Chain Operations in Retail

In the vast ecosystem of retail, supply chain operations often stand as vital but complex processes. As the lifeblood of retail, these operations are a network of entities, people, activities, information, and resources that deliver products or services from supplier to customer.

6.1. Understanding the Traditional Supply Chain

The traditional supply chain framework aims to manage the flow of goods and information, including sourcing the raw materials or goods, manufacturing or processing, storage, and distribution to the end consumer. These stages may seem linear, but they involve multiple entities such as producers, manufacturers, distributors, suppliers, transportation providers, and retailers. Critical issues of these operations not only relate to the logistical challenges but also include inefficiencies, lack of transparency, delays, and potential fraud.

6.2. The Advent of Retail 2.0 and Its Impact on Supply Chain

The sphere of retail is no longer what it once was. With technologically adept customers expecting faster deliveries, customized products, and transparency about products' journey, retail 2.0 is a paradigm shift. The advent of e-commerce and online marketplaces, rapid automation, and globalization have put pressure on traditional supply chain operations to revamp and respond to these massive shifts in consumer behaviors and expectations.

6.3. Blockchain: The Game Changer for Supply Chain Operations

Blockchain technology can serve as a potential solution to these problems by offering distinctive benefits in terms of security, traceability, and efficiency. Blockchain technology, at its core, is a decentralized digital ledger that records transactions across multiple computers so that any involved record cannot be altered retroactively, without the alteration of all subsequent blocks.

Blockchain's potential use in supply chain operations could fundamentally disrupt traditional processes by providing complete transparency and traceability. By harnessing this technology, retailers can ensure that transactions are secure, traceable, and free from interference.

6.4. Applying Blockchain in Retail Supply Chain: A Practical Approach

Blockchain technology can fortify the retail supply chain in several ways. First, let's explore the concept of "Provenance Tracking." Here, blockchain can offer a secure and immutable ledger that provides real-time visibility of items throughout the supply chain. It mitigates risks of counterfeit goods, delayed shipments, and frauds by tracing each transaction's history and granting access to relevant parties for verification.

Consider "Smart Contracts" – these self-executing contracts with the terms of agreement written into code. Blockchain could enable smarter and more efficient supply chains by automating processes usually prone to human error and delays. Instant payments, automatic warranties, delay penalties are all achievable with blockchain-backed smart contracts.

In terms of inventory management, blockchain can assist in reducing losses resulting from human error in inventory reporting. The use of IoT devices, paired with blockchain, can send real-time updates about inventory levels to the decentralized ledger, making stock management more accurate and reliable.

6.5. Case Study: Major Retailers Leveraging Blockchain

Walmart, a retail giant, has started using blockchain for traceability of certain food products. The ability to track food products' origins from farm to shelf in real-time has not only streamlined Walmart's operations but also significantly reduced the time required for food safety procedures.`

All in all, the advent of blockchain in supply chain operations of retail businesses offers myriad opportunities for improvement and innovation. The technology promises not only efficiency and transparency but a resilience capable of dealing with the dynamic nature of modern retail. Yet, while blockchain offers many benefits, it's not without its challenges, including scalability and interoperability issues. Despite these, the future of retail supply chains indeed seems to be leaning towards blockchain – a pivot toward a more transparent and efficient retail world.

6.6. The Roadmap to Blockchain Implementation

Implementing blockchain into retail supply chains requires a strategic approach. Enterprises should begin by identifying the right use cases where blockchain can add significant value. Key considerations would include the need for data security and transparency, the capability for real-time updates, and responsibilities for maintaining the blockchain.

The next step would be to design the architecture of the system, considering factors like permissions, network type (public or private blockchain), and interoperability with other systems. Working with technology experts or blockchain consultants may be necessary at this stage.

Likewise, enterprises should emphasize developing a robust governance model that defines the roles and responsibilities of all nodes in the blockchain network. It's also important to promote collaboration between all supply chain stakeholders and to consistently iterate and test the blockchain system for best results.

So, while the possibilities seem almost endless, successful implementation depends on several interlinked factors. It signifies an optimistic era of technological transformation geared towards sophisticated and transparent supply chains and offers a promising glimpse into what may become a new standard for the retail industry.

That's the world of retail - reimagined and ripe with potential.

Chapter 7. Revolutionizing Supply Chain Management with Blockchain

The transformation of supply chain management (SCM) begins, surprisingly, with the humble ledger book. For thousands of years, merchants have relied on ledgers to record transactions and keep track of their goods. With the advent of blockchain, this concept is elevated into a digital domain where it offers enormous potential to revolutionize supply chain management.

7.1. The Basics of Blockchain

Blockchain, at its core, is a decentralized and distributed digital ledger system. It is designed in such a way that it records transactions across several computers so that any involved record cannot be altered retroactively, without the alteration of all subsequent blocks. This gives it a high degree of security and makes it virtually immune to fraud.

Transactions on the blockchain are verified by a network of computers (or nodes), making the system self-regulating. Once a block of data is recorded on the blockchain, it's extremely difficult to change that data because it would require the consensus of the majority of the network, making blockchain a highly secure technology.

7.2. How Blockchain Enhances Supply Chains

Typical supply chains are complex, involving numerous parties from the producer to the consumer. Traditional systems lack transparency, which can lead to inefficiency, waste, and fraud.

Enter blockchain. By applying blockchain technology to supply chains, we can create a permanent, transparent record of a product's journey from start to finish. This opens up a range of possibilities:

Traceability: Understanding the origin and the journey of a product becomes simple with blockchain as every transaction and movement of the product across the supply chain is recorded on a permanent ledger.

Transparency: All participants of a blockchain network can view the entire history of transactions, bringing unparalleled transparency to the supply chain.

Security: Due to the decentralized and immutable nature of blockchain, records on the chain are safe from tampering and fraud.

7.3. Practical Applications of Blockchain in Supply Chain

To appreciate the real-world impact of blockchain technology, let's consider its role in several key areas of supply chain management.

Food Supply Chain: Blockchain can greatly improve food safety. By providing full visibility into the food supply chain, it can help identify sources of contamination quickly, minimizing harm and facilitating the recall process.

Pharmaceutical Supply Chain: With the immutable nature of blockchain, counterfeit or expired drugs can be easily identified and prevented from entering the supply chain.

Textile Industry: Blockchain allows for the verification of sustainable and ethical practices by tracking materials from their point of origin.

7.4. Enabling Smart Contracts

Smart contracts are self-executing contracts with the terms of the agreement directly written into code. They allow credible transactions to be carried out without third parties. These transactions are trackable and irreversible. Blockchain enables the functionality of smart contracts enhancing the ease of executing transactions in supply chain management.

7.5. The Future of Blockchain and Supply Chain Management

The integration of blockchain into supply chains is still at an early stage. Numerous businesses, however, are testing the waters, attracted by the potential benefits of increased transparency, traceability, and efficiency.

While the initial investment into blockchain technology can be significant, long-term savings and the potential for more secure, transparent business practices likely outweigh the costs. As improvements in technology further lower the barrier to entry, expect to see an increasing number of firms exploring and adopting blockchain to streamline their supply chains.

Integration of artificial intelligence with blockchain technology also represents a future avenue for exploration. This could lead to the creation of intelligent blockchain networks that can make automatic decisions to improve the efficiency of supply chains further, creating what might be termed the intelligent supply chain.

There's no denying the paradigm shift the advent of blockchain brings to supply chain management. Retailers who recognize the potential and take steps to incorporate blockchain into their operations will place themselves at the forefront of a historic change in the way supply chains are managed.

Chapter 8. Case Studies: Successful Blockchain Application in Retail

The retail industry, like a chameleon, is known for its adaptability to digital innovation. One such innovation is blockchain technology, an encrypted distributed database concept that has gained ground. Its successful implementation in Retail serves as not just a groundbreaking example but also as a learning aid for other sectors.

8.1. Blockchain in Retail: Walmart's Experiment

Walmart, a global leader in retail, decided to apply blockchain for tracking its products, right from the source to the shelf. The company collaborated with IBM to develop a blockchain-powered system that tracked two products, mangoes in the US and pork in China. These pilot projects demonstrated the potential of blockchain to provide end-to-end traceability across the supply chain.

Identifying the origin of a box of mangoes, which used to take around 7 days pre-blockchain, was reduced to 2.2 seconds. This ability to track the supply chain real-time was instrumental in ensuring the safety and authenticity of the products. Blockchain rendered a transparent system that could efficiently handle product recalls if required, enhancing customers' trust.

8.2. De Beers: Diamond Tracking

Diamond giant De Beers implemented blockchain to prove their diamonds were conflict-free, naturally-mined, and authentic. Dubbed

"Tracr," the system tracked diamonds from the mine to the retailer, ensuring full transparency and authenticity. Each diamond was assigned a unique identification code that recorded attributes like carat, clarity, and color onto the blockchain.

Tracr was a revolution, attracting retailers such as Signet Jewelers for the increased transparency it offered. With blockchain, De Beers had turned a challenging task into an efficient system that was transparent, traceable, and tamper-proof.

8.3. Alibaba: Tackling Counterfeit Goods

Chinese e-commerce giant Alibaba introduced blockchain to fight counterfeit luxury goods on its platform. The company developed a unique tamper-proof system where each product was assigned a unique ID that was recorded in the blockchain.

The partnership between Alibaba, PwC, and logistic companies allowed for a comprehensive product journey, from the manufacturer to the end consumer. Customers could scan a QR code on the products to determine the origins and journey of the purchased goods. This innovation significantly reduced counterfeit products and increased consumer trust in Alibaba.

8.4. JD.com: Ensuring Food Safety

JD.com, another leading e-commerce company in China, collaborated with Intercontinental Hotels to create a blockchain application to track meat supply. The system traced the entire supply chain, including breeders, processors, transportation, and hotels.

Clients, by scanning a QR code, could access information on food origin, diet of the livestock, and storage temperatures. JD's blockchain implementation greatly increased supply chain transparency, enhancing consumer confidence and establishing a model for the future.

8.5. Auchan: Long-term Farming-focused blockchain project

Auchan, a French multinational retail company, implemented blockchain technology through the "TE-FOOD" project to track its products from farm to stores. Customers could scan a QR code on the products to get detailed information about the farming, slaughtering, and transportation processes.

Auchan's blockchain project marked one of the most extensive food safety data integrations and stood as a testament to the possibilities of blockchain capabilities.

8.6. Conclusion

The successful implementation of blockchain in these retail giants serves to demonstrate the power of blockchain technology for transparency, traceability, and enhanced customer confidence. These case studies have designed a paradigm showing how blockchain can be leveraged to track product from their origin, fight counterfeit, and ensure safety, all factors ultimately leading to improved customer experience.

The adaptability of these retailers to assimilate blockchain in their operations is a cue for others. While the road to blockchain adoption might seem complex, the potential that it holds for the retail world is groundbreaking and it's just waiting to be harnessed. By leveraging blockchain technology, retailers can improve their supply chains, increase transparency, and create a shopping environment that earns customer trust, a matter of paramount importance in the hyper-competitive world of Retail.

Chapter 9. Challenges and Solutions: Implementing Blockchain in Retail

Blockchain technology, while impressive and truly ground-breaking, does not come without its set of challenges, particularly in the retail sector. However, coupled with these challenges are innovative solutions that are powering the successful integration of blockchain in the industry. This chapter confronts these challenges head-on, offering both understanding and pragmatic solutions.

9.1. Understanding and Education

Oscillating between hype and skepticism, many are left confused about what blockchain is, how it works and what benefits it can bring to the retail industry. This lack of understanding often creates a reluctance in businesses to adopt this nascent technology.

Solution: Retail businesses must invest in education and training programs to facilitate comprehension and promote adoption among their employees. Simultaneously, they should focus on educating their customers about the benefits of blockchain technology, such as enhanced security, greater transparency, and improved efficiency.

9.2. Generating Buy-In

Often, the top echelons of a business remain skeptical about the practicality and advantages of blockchain. This skepticism, combined with heavyweight inertia, can slow progress and impede implementation.

Solution: Demonstrating successful use-cases aligns with intuitive understanding and generates trust in the technology. Companies in the retail sector need to highlight and articulate the successes already achieved by blockchain integration to their upper management and stakeholders.

9.3. Regulatory Concerns

Regulatory landscapes worldwide are highly variable, often unclear, and are playing catch-up with blockchain technology. This lack of clarity creates uncertainty that can deter businesses from adopting blockchain.

Solution: It's essential for retailers to closely follow and engage with the ongoing development of blockchain-oriented regulations and guidelines. Retailers can also involve legal and financial advisors to navigate complex regulations while planning their blockchain implementation strategy.

9.4. Technological Compatibility

Given the established nature of many retail businesses, integrating an innovative technology like blockchain might prove challenging with pre-existing IT infrastructure.

Solution: It would be beneficial to work with teams of software and IT specialists who are familiar with blockchain. They could ensure the compatibility of blockchain technology with existing systems or outline a well-devised plan to upgrade the current infrastructure to facilitate integration.

9.5. Consensus Model Selection

Blockchain operates on consensus models, which are protocols that ensure all transactions are validated by network participants.

Choosing a model that aligns with a company's needs can be challenging due to factors like security, speed, and transparency.

Solution: Different business needs require different consensus models. Therefore, evaluating business needs, understanding the pros and cons of each consensus model, consulting with blockchain experts, and testing various models would be the best approach.

9.6. Dealing with Scalability

With blockchain, there's a trade-off between decentralization and scalability. As the number of transactions increases, it becomes challenging for the network to remain decentralized and maintain its performance.

Solution: Retail businesses can explore scaling solutions, such as sharding or off-chain transactions. Sharding involves creating smaller, manageable parts of the network, while off-chain transactions reduce the load on the main chain. Both solutions ensure high throughput without compromising the core benefits of decentralization.

9.7. Privacy Concerns

By design, blockchain technology provides transparency and security. However, the transparency feature could also be a concern for businesses working with confidential information.

Solution: The advanced concept of 'Zero Knowledge Proofs' can be employed, which enables transaction validation without revealing any specifics. Privacy-centric blockchains, like Zcash or Monero, are also worth considering for retailers.

The runway to integrating blockchain into retail businesses may be littered with challenges, but identifying hurdles and understanding solutions to overcome them can ensure a smooth landing. With proper planning, education, and continuous monitoring of the evolving landscape, blockchain technology could feasibly revolutionize retail.

Chapter 10. Future Perspectives: Blockchain Trends in the Retail Industry

Blockchain technology has made the leap from mere buzzword into the realm of concrete applicability. As we gaze into the future, it's clear that blockchain's transformative impact in the retail industry will continue to evolve and ripple outward, disrupting the way we traditionally understand retail operations.

10.1. Blockchain as the Backbone of Supply Chain

In the retail industry, efficient supply chain management is mission-critical. Blockchain's ability to facilitate more transparent and secure transactions lends itself to forging strong links in the supply chain. At its simplest, blockchain operates as a decentralized ledger that logs and verifies all transactions linearly. Errors, fraud, or discrepancies become easier to locate and rectify. When combined with IoT (Internet of Things) technology, which shares data across a network of internet-connected devices, blockchain further acts as a source of real-time information about any linked item's status.

Forward-looking retailers have already started implementing blockchain systems into their supply chains. For example, to verify the legality and sustainability of the products, blockchain can be leveraged to track the journey of a product from the source to the consumer. This not only enhances supply chain efficacy but also promotes transparency, allowing consumers to make informed decisions about what they buy and from whom.

10.2. Transformation in Payment Methods

In finance, blockchain is often familiarly linked to cryptocurrencies such as Bitcoin. These cryptocurrencies provide alternative modes of payment that are decentralized, secure, faster, and efficient. Gradually, cryptocurrencies have started to make their way into retail payment modes. Retailers such as Overstock.com and Shopify have begun to accept Bitcoin payments, pointing towards an emerging trend.

In the future, as more people adopt cryptocurrencies and as their acceptance increases globally, we can expect a significant transformation in the way payments occur within retail. As blockchain eliminates the need for intermediaries in financial transactions, retailers can potentially enjoy lower transaction costs with cryptocurrencies, a trend which, if adopted widely, could influence pricing strategies in retail dramatically.

10.3. Personalization & Customer Experience

It's no secret that personalization drives customer engagement, and hence, sales. With blockchain, retailers can avail the benefits of decentralized customer data, allowing for more precisely targeted marketing. As blockchain makes it possible to store data securely, it provides avenues for customers to share their information with brands they trust. Thus, blockchain has the potential to build a relationship based on trust between consumers and retailers resulting in deeper personalization.

10.4. Counterfeit Product Reduction

Counterfeit products pose issues for brands and consumers alike, denting brand reputation and sales. Blockchain comes in handy here. Thanks to the secure and transparent nature of blockchain, every product could, in theory, sport a blockchain "tag", verifying its authenticity and origin. This could lead to a significant reduction in counterfeit products in the future. Blockchain can, in essence, help build trust across the transactional chain, from brands to consumers.

10.5. Improving Warranty Management

Warranties often involve tedious paperwork, which can be misplaced, causing problems when it's needed. Blockchain technology can come to the rescue here as the warranty information can be stored in a blockchain, making it easy to access while reducing the risk of fraudulent claims.

10.6. Social and Environmental Impact

Increasingly, consumers urge retailers to demonstrate their commitment to social causes and sustainable practices. By offering traceability throughout the entire chain of custody, blockchain can provide detailed information about a product's origin, how it was created, its environmental footprint, and more. This transparency can support sustainable and ethical retail practices, strengthening brand loyalty among conscious consumers.

In conclusion, the future of retail looks set to be greatly impacted by blockchain technology. Its many applications, such as transparent supply chains, safer payment systems, personalized customer experiences, counterfeit reduction, improved warranty and after-sales service, and support for ethical business practices, are transformative. Retailers who begin to explore these blockchain-based opportunities now will potentially reap the benefits of a technologically empowered retail scenario in the not-so-distant future.

Chapter 11. Your Next Steps: A Practical Guide to Leveraging Blockchain

The journey towards leveraging blockchain in retail starts with an understanding of the technology's capabilities, followed by a tailored implementation approach that suits your unique business needs. Here's a step-by-step guide to help you unfold this transformative journey.

11.1. Recognize the Potential of Blockchain

Blockchain, at its simplest, is a distributed and secure digital ledger that maintains integrity by recording transactions across multiple computers. It's the technology behind crypto-currencies like Bitcoin but it can do far more than just support cryptocurrency.

For retailers, blockchain can unlock the potential for increased transparency, heightened security, and streamlined operations. This is achieved through the capability of blockchain to provide unalterable records, traceability of products, and smart contracts which can automate various transactions. But how does it apply to your retail business operationally? The first thing you need is a clear assessment of where you can leverage blockchain the most.

11.2. Assess Blockchain Opportunities

Begin by identifying operational areas where blockchain could bring significant improvements. This includes supply chain management where the technology can improve traceability and combat counterfeiting; customer loyalty programs where blockchain can facilitate rewards and redemption; and payments where the technology can streamline transactions and reduce fraud.

Work closely with your team, discussing and identifying potential use cases. Having a clear understanding of how blockchain could be beneficial is the first step in your journey.

11.3. Assemble a Capable Team

Implementing blockchain is no small undertaking. It requires a team of experts who are familiar with the technology. Consider building a diverse internal team of IT professionals, retail operations specialists, and business strategists, or partnering with a reputable blockchain consulting firm. The aim here is to collaborate and bring diverse thoughts and angles to the project.

The team will be responsible for developing a strategic plan, defining the scope of work, identifying potential challenges and coming up with solutions.

11.4. Understand Your Blockchain Options

There are several types of blockchains, such as public, private and consortium. Public and private blockchains are either open to everyone or exclusively controlled by your organization respectively. Consortium or federated blockchains involve several organizations sharing the control. Depending on your specific needs, the governance model of your blockchain network may vary.

Alongside, it's essential to explore available blockchain platforms. Some of the more well-known include Ethereum, Hyperledger Fabric, IBM Blockchain, and R3 Corda. Each platform has its strengths. For example, Ethereum's Smart Contract functionality is superior, while Hyperledger is known for its operational efficiency and modularity.

11.5. Develop a Proof of Concept

A Proof of Concept (PoC) provides a practical demonstration of how blockchain would work in your organization. It's an opportunity to test the feasibility and efficacy of blockchain before undertaking a full-scale implementation.

During this stage, your team would simulate a reduced scale version of the envisioned blockchain implementation. Monitor closely, seek feedback, analyze results, and refine the approach accordingly. This will pave the way for a smoother, more effective blockchain rollout.

11.6. Roll Out the Pilot Implementation

Once you've completed the PoC, the next step is to launch a pilot project. This should be implemented on a larger scale than the PoC but is still not a full-scale, organization-wide rollout. Again, the key here is monitoring and feedback.

The experiences and insights derived from the pilot stage will be instrumental in fine-tuning your final implementation plan.

11.7. Scaling Up

Now, it's time to launch your full-scale implementation. With your knowledge and preparation from the PoC and pilot, your team should be prepared to drive the blockchain implementation with confidence.

The rollout should be done carefully, with potential fallback options at your disposal to cater for any unexpected outcomes. It is also a good practice to keep stakeholders aware of your progress, milestones, and any barriers or hurdles confronted during the implementation.

11.8. Make Continuous Improvements

Post-implementation, the journey doesn't end. The process of evolution and change in blockchain is consistent. Learn from the experiences, study user behavior, and keep introducing improvements. Be receptive to innovations and advancements in the field of blockchain, ensure your solution remains future-proof.

In summary, integrating blockchain into your retail operation is not an overnight process, but a strategic journey. It demands careful planning, expert resources, detailed execution, and persistent improvements. But the long-term benefits are worth all the efforts: better transparency, higher security, streamlined transactions, and most importantly a tremendous customer experience. Leverage blockchain's potential - it might be the breakthrough technology your retail business has been waiting for.